CIRCLE OF BLUE

Quarantine Learning

Published By

Quarantine Learning (Circle of blue)

Edited By Sujata Nayak

Published by : Poetry World Org.

Publisher's Address : Haryana

 Special credits to Dr.Niveditha and Dr.Nitin Chopra.

Edition : I (2021)

ISBN (Paperback) - 9789390724659

Book Design by POETRY WORLD

CIRCLE OF BLUE

Quarantine Learning

Compiler & editor

Sujata Nayak

COMPILER

She is a passionate writer. As she is an introvert, she expresses herself by penning down her thoughts. She believes in subconscious power strongly & inspires peoples to develop an optimistic outlook towards their life.

Avocation- Dance, Artist, crafts, sporty fellow, explorer, photography. Being an astute, she often observes the things out & finds answers to her messed up thoughts by staring deep inside the valley of her thoughts & inspire the readers to explore themselves.

Email- suznay8@gmail.com

Instagram handle- @suju_nayak

BOON FOR NATURE, BANE FOR HUMANS

"Change is the law of universe. What you think of as death, indeed life. In one instance you can sleep on bed of money and in other instance, you can be steeped into poverty. Yours & mine, big & small - erase this ideas from your mind. Then everything is yours & you belong to everyone."

- By Lord Krishna

All predictions & estimations are not in our hands now. The world has become volatile. CoVid-19 has risen as something new, phenomenal & nobody has any thought of it. One thing is sure; nothing will ever be same again. Nothing is permanent. From the beginning of this pandemic, we have seen & still are seeing many changes both good & bad, here & there everywhere. This situation can be considered as the example of 2 sides of a coin. If the huge impact of outbreak on the economy at large, including loss of daily wage workers to millions of those in unorganized sector, the lockdown implemented have come as blessing in disguise to the power distribution companies running in loss. Whereas it proves good for poor and rich, the middle class people were worst hit. The poor were provided with relief & many more facilities according to different norms.

The rich people have such money that they could sit in home & eat whatever they want whereas middle class people who were struggling daily to get some are deprived of the same due to lockdown which proved to be a headache for them.

As the disease & lockdown spread, the environment changed in the sky above our heads, the air in our lungs & even ground beneath our feet. While human toll mounted vigorously from a single case in Wuhan to a global pandemic, nature, it seemed, was increasingly able to breathe more easily. As the motorway cleared, factories closed pollution but shrunk over cities & industrial carters in country after country. Dozens of countries experienced temporary fall in CO_2 & NO_2 improving air quality & reducing risks of asthma, heart attacks & lung disease. Air traffic halved & road traffic fell. The human footprint on the earth suddenly seemed lightened with less human movement, the planet has literally calmed.

With fewer drivers on roads and planes in air, the price of oil has clumped. Some marked it start of a prolonged downward trend in emissions & beginning of the end for oil as oil is the biggest sources of carbon emission which disrupts the weather systems. Air pollution has plunged in many ideas. While human lost their jobs, nature became millionaire.

**Nature's bounce back*

With less human interferences, nature heals better. Scientists reported lower vibrations from 'cultural noise'. The toll for road kill by cars & trucks are lowered which in UK alone- annually takes the lives of about 100,000 hedgehogs, 30,000 deers, 100,000 foxes. Wild boar became bolder in Barcelona & Bergamo, Italy. In Wales peacock have strutted through Bangor, goats through Llandudno & sheep have been seemed on roundabouts in deserted playground in Monmouthshire. There's clear water all over Venice, blue skies over Delhi, Himalayas seen from Punjab & animals seen roaming freely in lockdown, but the grim reality is, these changes are temporal.

Cartoonists depict throngs of tourists' animals gawping through city windows at humans under lockdown. Humour doesn't get much blacker. Humans laughed at their own decline & assumingly that nature will be beneficiary.

**Is nature's comeback worth celebrating?*

It's been over everywhere that "Nature has hit the reset button", but will these changes be actually boon for the environment? This is a temporary healing moment for the nature, as emission will raise higher when economic activities gain momentum. "Nature is healing". Yes, it is. But it's not the planned way to heal the nature. It's not the humans who helped the nature to bounce back. Clearly, it's not something 'to celebrate'.

Environmental campaigners said that it's a dangerous misconception. Rich, industrialized nations are seeing a temporary recovery of the nature because there is so little of it in first phase. Poorer countries on the other hand, in southern hemisphere, fear an increased threat to wildlife because pandemic means they have less money & personnel to conserve endangered species & habitats. In the Masai Mara & Serengeti, nature reserves are taking less tourists' revenue, which means they are struggling to pay rangers. Conservation groups started fearing that this will open the door to more illegal poaching, mining & logging, especially, as local people are losing income & need new ways to feed their families.

INDEX

AN EPIC STORY

Shreya Gardas

"An epic story, but don't worry.
Its corona to fight,
A tales says a lot."
"All of a sudden everything forbidden.

It sounds Corona
Like a creeper, this reached people like a monster.
Make us panic, created a pandemic.
To face this virus, we have to sanitize.
To avoid the risk, we have to wear a mask.
Not just once, but washing our hands twice or thrice.

They declared ""LOCKDOWN""
When we were just sitting at home.
And warriors left their home.
Doctors and nurses,
Police and municipality workers,
Government and guardians.
Worked hard, struggled a lot.
Served the nation following their profession.
Where they work on a mission,
Some lost home, some lost food.
Some lost money, many lost their life.
Some got stuck, some were sick.
To stay safe, we have to stay home.
Show some humanity, ensure safety.

LOCKDOWN LEARNING

Venkat Singh

"It was the first time for all of us to be in a home arrest,
First it felt like life is falling apart and looked all messed,
But staying home is the only way to fight.
Every day seems like its Sunday,
For entertainment we all find one or the other way,
Being a helping hand to do household work with mom,
Feeling her sacrifices she does to run the house but still she's calm.
Sensing the tension for the money to run the house and to pay bills,
Dad never showed his dark side his struggle and never made we feel.
After spending the time with the grandparents, mom and dad,
Listening their stories what they did, how they lived and what they had,
The months have passed by the same routine only.
But like the normal days we weren't lonely.
This pandemic made us learn the value of life, health, money and many more things.
The world tested positive for Covid by staying outside,

Meanwhile we learned to deal with life with positivity by staying inside.
Real life requires a limited resource to live,
Only the showoff life needs a huge amount of money, this pandemic made us believe.
We all have learnt a lot of things in these Lockdown days,
All hidden talents came out of the hays,
Yeah there were many negative incidences too in all those time,
But somehow we managed to chill and enjoy without the wine.
It showed us what real life is and how to deal with it,
It also made us learn we can live alone and solve out our problems without creating any shit.
The Lockdown is over but not the Covid,
So please kindly take the precautions one day the world will get rid of it.

ALONE

Lamiya Siraj

Not Alone yet Had to be Left All 'ALONE' "Past last one year I have been dreaming of my Wedding Day! The day I saw her, I knew it was her for whom I had been waiting for. Her smile and innocence captivated my heart in our first meeting arranged at our home. Yes, I am coming from an Indian family wherein the trend of 'Arranged Marriages' are still ON. Understanding the outlook for life and plans we had we know we are the best choice to set examples for future generation as of 'MADE FOR EACH OTHER'! We belong to two different states of INDIA. Yet we choose to walk together the path of the married life without knowing the destination leaving it on our destiny.

This year when the Covid-19 hit the entire world, a lot of things changed with the virus, lockdowns and pandemic all around. Plans were cancelled & shuffled according to situations. I come under both these categories. My Marriage was fixed after two years in 2022 but the situation arose in such a way that we had to take it up this year. So, November 2020 was finalized in June 2020 keeping in hand at least five months for all preparations following protocols as per the Government guidelines.

November came! I was excited. I took leave for a week. Morning while going to saloon I felt uneasy and feverish. Without a second thought or delay I went and took Covid-19 test and came positive! Ah, that was the end of the day as I was broken emotionally and could see a storm of emotions coming from my family members. The next day we had confirmed tickets of flight for around 15 family members. Everything came to a halt all sudden.

I was now in the pool of tears; one side was my mother whom I had to assure, and worst part was I was in front of her yet closed in a separate room now. She could only see me and talk from a safe distance. The thing killing us both was my whole life whenever I felt sick, she used to take me on her lap, make me sleep and be by my side all the time till I recovered completely. But this was the first time I was in front of her eyes, yet she couldn't come near to me or touch me! And the other side was my going to be 'BETTER HALF'. This news to her also became a disaster as I understand all preparations were done and we were weaving our dreams for our Wedding-Day for the past six months!

Apart from this I had to assure answering entire family members staying apart from them locked up in one room declaring yes, I am doing well!

It took me fourteen long days, and by the grace of GOD my reports came negative. Once again it was the time to achieve our dream. So, we fulfilled it finally by saying 'QABOOL HAI'!

LOCKDOWN

Jayashree Sahoo

This lockdown is not just lock for me
It's my freedom to flying in my own world by dancing, singing just for cherishing my life.
Still, there some lack of my friends my teachers, my classmates, my best friend and my hostel also.
I'm missing them very much, though I see them on zoom, Google meet or video call in what Sapp,
Still I'm missing their presence on my surroundings.
It's this lockdown time, where I thought that
I'll try to put a smile on those peoples who sacrifices their life for my growing and glowing,
I tried my best to happier them by my little jokes and funny dancing videos.
Where in hostel, I just spend my family time with voice call, but there no deter for spending more time in this lockdown which giving full of enormous glee.

POSITIVE THINKING ABOUT LOCKDOWN

Debesh Prusty

"Eventually, everyone quarantined to their house for nearly six month it is not so easy to accept that but it happened. Everything is theoretically impossible, until it is done. We never supposed to accept that there is going to be a situation where we will just stay in home no vacation no work no freedom to go outside just like we are prisoners in our own house.

Sometimes things get worse before they get better. Positive thinking will let you do everything than negative thinking. May be it was a pandemic time, everyone faced problems but in a positive way we enjoyed a cheerful and peaceful moments with our family which we can't give our family because of busy life. This pandemic gives us the opportunity to spend time with our family.

Look for something positive in your everyday, even if someday you have to look a little harder."

LETTER TO THE UNSEEN VIRUS

Nivetha R C

Could you please wear the mask?
Only one thing became our task.
"Rest in peace good soul" are the words heard a lot.
“One by one" reminisced the school days that we forgot
News channel telecasted for 24 hours
Additionally, we started taking showers.

Video calls with friends carried a bunch of emotions
I'm in the hospital" painted minds with commotions.
Result is negative was the only positive thing
Uniformed people's virtue made us not to blink.
Staying in the home was the foremost solution

Praying for the lives became our unwritten resolution
Am I audible?" made us wake
Network issue served as a way to escape
Drinking hot water evolved us the unsaid prescription
Even handshaking served a way for transmission
Many pages in 2020 diary filled up with blanks
In-depth it carried a silent message of thanks
Corona all this happened because of you.
But I request you to stop taking lives with you.

LOCKDOWN LIFE

Gautam Kumar

(2020) A decade started and it is obvious it started after 10years and the globe is under a harsh conditions of pandemic, chaos, rumors and a lot of such things which are creating hodgepodge. We (Indians) as per the documents and database are taking requisite preventing methods to keep ourselves safe i.e. social distancing but things I am not being able to understand inspite of these preventing measures, lightning diyas, switching on and off the lights of our houses, beating the utensils like musicians assuming them some technological advanced musical instruments the number of Corona patients are increasing dramatically each day.

Even chanting and the universal medicine Gaumutra (of which our intellectual minds were boasting of too much) seems like outdated in front of this tiny virus. The number of Corona patients is increasing dramatically across the globe. The best line I know from the field of medical sciences is that "Prevention is better than cure" and amidst this pandemic it seems only possible solution at hand right now as there is no vaccine at present. One of the best possible solutions to avoid (this inevitable seeming pandemic) the risk of contamination from this tiny virus is Lockdown.

It literally means, "An emergency measures or condition in which people are temporarily prevented from entering or leaving a restricted areas or building" but in present situation from home. We all know this is the best possible steps to be taken but you can't simply ignore the consequences of anything you do whether it's your choice or action and similarly it has put hazardous impacts especially to the laborers, poor family, economy of a country, education and so on. The list is a way longer. We ought to face the consequences as it was sudden burst like most of time, time does these in our lives and provide the guidance to take lessons from those things but being the most careless species of this planet despite having so much advanced brain, complex structure have never tried to learn lessons from the nature.

Inspite of all the difficulties lockdown has caused or is causing to the people, a country or the globe it has taught us various priceless lessons. The greatest one is that we should always remain to ready to shape ourselves according to the nature as it is the ultimate things we are for , or are because of since the nature itself is not going to compromise in either way. Lockdown has taught us to be socially connected while following the preventive measures like social distancing and proper hygiene and cleanliness through advanced technologies of which some of our intellectual minds used to disregard as this is not going to help us and is going to only increase the distance between people, community and nature.

But now, we can easily figure out, what is the main factor which is providing the way to get or be connected with people? Continuing our education? I agree that only the digital way to teach or study is not much worth in comparison to the conventional way as the digital media will allow you to access information, get data, sources, and a lot more things but simply it can't help you to learn. But still is the best source during this period of catastrophe and lockdown. I have seen various people complaining about the problems they are facing because of lockdown and how distraught they have grown. I know the problem is inevitable but still you can find the hidden opportunity and positive sides of the problem if you look it carefully.

Let me clarify you, if you are one of them complaining guy, or one from the distraught, disturbed, frustrated guys who is not able to visit the planned places or something like this or you are one who are feeling bored from oneself! There can't be much ironical situation than to be bored with oneself. Then, think about the one who don't have choices, privilege like you, then you will feel grateful for what you have got.

Lockdown has remarkably showed us that the process of healing if nature is quite rapid as we can clearly notice or you might have noticed that the sky is being clear from pollution, water bodies have become crystal clear, glaciers and above of all the climate, rainfall has improved. Now I should talk about the priceless time we have got to spend sorry, utilize with our family. We all know that once you set your feet outside the home for anything whether it is for further studies, or work or anything similar you just became a guest as the time and situations will never be the same as it was used to be.

Let me share my personal experience, as the lockdown started I was literally happy that I got more holidays to enjoy but as it started to remain for longer period and yet longer period then I started feeling bored, started complaining about the things, without considering the other possible consequences as I was focusing only on the negative sides. But then I started to explore myself and my village and I concluded that both are a way more beautiful and mysterious full of elegant treasures I have beaver thought of Lockdown provided me the time to unbury the buried talents, shades of myself and compelled me to push the limit to higher extent in the same manner as the nature and our mother earth is doing for the benefit of themselves and the lives. Despite I forgot to bring some of my things that could be beneficial for the expenditure of time but I am happy that somehow I could boost my cooking skill, gardening, observations by observing the beauty of nature, it's aura, lessons, healing process and started figure out the answer to all the questions. The very best lesson I have learnt is about time.

One day (early days of lockdown), in the morning, I got up after the sunrise since the sunrays was falling on my face and also because no one has asked me to get up. I got fresher myself up and went into the kitchen in order to get something to eat as till then it was 10 O'clock and the sun was looking unusual brighter. I saw there was still late in the preparation of breakfast, I almost broke out in my mother but as I was about to burst I saw my mother very closely just like the chemists who observe his beaker in order to get some result or notice any unusual consequence of the reaction.

She was wearing a saree, was standing in front of the stoves, the beam of bright sun rays were falling on her head which was coming from the window and the just like the stream of river, the sweat has formed a stream for itself and was falling very slowly from the forehead towards the left cheek to the way to chin. I saw she is so beautiful and observed that the hair has started to grew grey, wrinkles have started to create their home on that beautiful face that has provided me the face, the lessons like generosity, respect and so many uncountable things and at the same time I say my father who was seating on a chair and was reading newspaper I observed his hair has started to become grey and fall at the same time and also that the half blue and white check shirt he was wearing seems loose which was used to be fit on him. At that moment I noticed the ageing process, the very thin line of time that goes slowly but smoothly and I realized that I am also under this process. There is no substitute of time and we ought to utilize it precisely and judicially.

THE CORONA HYPOCRITE

Bhargavi Vardhan

Leela was too busy with all the domestic chores at home. She had stopped going to work. Thanks to the lockdown and the fear of Corona infection with a newborn and an old ailing mother in law at home. Leela was a post graduate in microbiology. She knew too much about the virus to be carefree.

On the other hand Nakul was into government services. He had no choice on staying at home as he was in police department. And he was not really bothered because, "how can virus come into contact with him", he was being very careful. He was wearing a mask, taking bath when he came back home. And he had stopped his alcohol parties too. That's amazing. Right?

Leela would clean and sanitize everything that came home. She was doing everything to protect her family. No, she couldn't touch Nakul's things. Because you know, these were important things, and he was being too careful anyway.

Leela couldn't let any of her relatives visit their baby. They could be carriers of infection. Leela totally agreed. Because she knew too well that anyone could pass on the infection. But Nakul's relatives could see the baby.

They love the baby. And you know they are being too careful. They cannot pass on any infection. Leela was too scared at every such visit.

Nakul always consoled her saying that disease doesn't spread in villages, you see, only cities are infected. And on the top of it, theirs was the richest family in the village; the laborers at home would not dare to infect them.

In one such argument with Nakul, Leela was thrashed real hard with his lathi. And she was only too scared to protest against these visits now. Sometimes she felt like running away with her baby, but her parents were at the other end of the country. And they were too poor to take care of them anyway. Now all she could do is to pray and wait.

And one day, the old ailing mother in law suddenly collapsed. Nakul was too busy to take the emergency call. Leela rushed her to the hospital and had to leave the infant in the neighborhood.

Her mother in law passed away hours after they went to hospital with a breathing distress. All the family members came home for the last rites. She was the thakurain after all. In all these "inevitable" circumstances, the baby fell ill. He had a very high temperature. Nakul and Leela rushed him to the hospital, but the baby succumbed to breathlessness while he was in the emergency ward.

Leela was not able to understand anything. All she felt was her soul ripping apart from her body. Like someone was punishing her for her weaknesses. She was feeling the guilt of staying back. She wanted to shout out loud. But hardly anyone could hear her. She knew at that moment that she would leave Nakul. She would never be able to forgive him. He would never understand her plight. Never.

ATTENTION SEEKER

Mansi Gupta

You the attention seeker stoked our fear
"The lanes are deprived of laughter;
The roads have become deserted;
Mother Nature at her best,
Might be smiling for our fate.

These have made us to realize,
The virus does not discriminate between rich-poor, black-white, height-wide;
It's our own thought to fight.
Gods have closed their doors,
And humans are now each other's foe;
Humanity is to be claimed;
Are the religions to be blamed?

You the attention seeker stoked our fear.
The increasing number;
The lost loved ones;
The agony;
The emptiness uplifted the melancholy.
The fine knot of
Patience and strength, is swiftly parted.

Yes, you COVID-19;
The global pandemic has dragged well beyond our limits.

LOCKDOWN: THE TRAGIC BUT MAGICAL JOURNEY

Dhanya Ravi

"A lovely couple got married recently by exchanging their promise to make love forever. As days passed, there aroused some unexpected changes in this new phase of life to both of them. The girl started adjusting, accepting and understanding the changes around her. The guy was trying hard to make sure everything is fine. But don't know why, for some reason they weren't living a life they wished. Their decisions were rejected, their actions were questioned and their small wishes were not understood and finally their dreams were shattered because of others.

So, they decided with heavy heart to go little away and do something to prove the people their decision is right and the path they chose is absolutely fine. But then, the innocent couple didn't know the upcoming entry of tragedy into their life. The couple started a travel with dreams to chase with only love whole heartedly. But there came so much twists and turns. The travel was fine, but his people around there had different plans for him. Once he understood that only money matters not passion he didn't want to continue there. The couple plan to go back home.

The extreme twist aroused in the name of "corona" a virus arrived. The couple with self-respect as first priority anyways decided to leave the place with their heart broken, because of the fake people's act. The journey was at high difficulty but reached home safe and they could finally breathe with a relief. At this point, the couple lost all their savings in name of travel expense. The coming back didn't give them everything back as before.

The so called " lockdown" announced for safeguarding the people. This was an unexpected pause in their life which made them confused with no ways ahead. But the lovely couple collected all the bad memories that other people threw at them for moving forward and decided to go ahead with not tears but with a positive smile. At that moment they may not be financially wealthy, but they had each other to shower love and hold hands to support in these toughest times. The lockdown, the stress, the work loses, financial crisis, Debts, EMI, rent and on the top of it, the people ditched, all those harsh words and what not?? The days passing but nothing is standing still all these responsibilities wandering them around. But they didn't put head down and sit and cry.

They supported each other's work passion, ideas and enjoyed even these worst moments with all these struggles and overcame everything with just confidence and love. The lockdown in some way or other helped them also, to understand them and each other better, to learn new things, to take a break from hectic lifestyle, to be away from unwanted things and the toxic people affecting their peace of mind.

Now the girl started taking steps to develop her passion and the guy is supporting her in all possible ways and encouraging her. The guy learned and developed skills with his passion and continued his works with all dedication. With all hard work and determination, they moved ahead and succeeded gradually. They started to slowly get back to normal life. The gradually became firm on financial basis and they also proved and proving they were right to everyone.

The lesson learnt from lockdown are plenty? Lockdown was a boon and a curse for them. But if we think and try, we can overcome the curse and make it a blessing and use it for our betterment like the lovely couple did. Their journey from then till now wasn't smooth, it was amidst a roller coaster ride, fast and furious too.

So, everyone worrying on past over incidents and the toxic people are of no use. Sitting idle and blaming the situation around us, has nothing to do in our life. Don’t lose hope on yourself, be confident. Just live your life by changing all odds on your way into positive way.

SPREAD LOVE, SPREAD POSITIVITY.

TEACHINGS OF LOCKDOWN

Harshita Garg

Lockdown taught us a lot. 2020 has been the most unexpected and weird year we were all been through and now this year will go to end soon. Worldwide lockdown has made people stay at one place and carry out the work they have been pending for a long time.

Apart from so much of negative happenings in this year, there something positive as well. Learning. Yes, you heard it right. 2020 has taught us the value of the thing we were least important to us but now we are surviving due to it. I learnt a lot from this lockdown and I have included these points in my lockdown dairy-

- Never underestimate your health
- Don't just learn about to earn money, learn how to multiply it
- Work on building your skills and if you are good at that, don't work for free
- Learning work from home, managing personal and professional life, and trying new things
- Free time should be utilized wisely

Unexpected and unwanted things often realize the true value of important things in our life. Lockdown was one of them. Spending family time at home, learning to cook various tasty dishes, celebrating the everyday, improving your professional skills and gaining practical experience while working from home, all are invaluable experiences that we can't forget anytime soon. Thus, I would like to end this small story of mine on a positive note that doesn't be afraid to try out new things and always believe that if others can, you can also achieve it.

QUARANTINE WORLD

Anil Kumar Prajapati

"Quarantine now became the world
Cause made for employment
How many people are left hungry?
And how many of their fathers have died.

Tandav was created by corona
And employment was going to end
Labor was going helpless
Reaching the sad news of everyone at home.

Now money was going to end on pockets
And market was shut down
They had no food for eating
Poor people walked on foot.

Labor was arriving at house
And people were forcing them
People were treating likes
As it was their fault.

Now Quarantine is going over
And everyday life is coming back on track
That news is making happy to everyone
And we will got thousands new type of jobs.

REALIZATION

Swarnika Saha

"Self-love is salient, I realized then
Everyone treated me as a trespasser
Whenever I want to meet them.
I told them all, I wasn't Covid positive
But suddenly all started to behave
As if I was a person full of lurgies.
Situations revealed the phiz of them,
Whenever I asked for a help from them.
Quarantine made me realize that
You are salient to no one
Except your God gifted parents,
Who work hard day and night?
To keep up your lavish existence.
Self-love is important, I realized then
Never crave to die for that person
Who don't even try to care?
Never crave to die for someone
Who doesn't even need your care?"

A BITTER-SWEET YEAR

Arrisa Shahpriya Sur

"It was a Monday morning. I woke up to a beautiful, bright sunny day. I checked my phone. I was late for school. I barely had time to have breakfast, put on some clothes, and rush. It was always my mom's yelling that helped me reach school on time.

At school, it was another normal day. Classes are all lined up, recess, and friends of course. I distinctly remember that it was the 15th of March and the Covid19 news flashed on every news channel. As we all dispersed, our teacher told us that our classes would not commence the next day onwards.

I wondered why. My dad then told me that the deadly virus has hit the whole world. I was curious about how it started and asked him. He told me that a person in China had eaten a bat. The bat was a carrier and had managed to infect the man. It was a new virus and so there no cure.

The virus had started spreading at an amazingly scary speed! I was banned from going to play with friends. I couldn't even step out of the house. One thing I noticed was that our pollution levels drastically dropped down. No one wanted to risk their lives so they stayed at home. No one took their cars out! To top it off since the whole world was on lockdown no one was coming to our house to help with the cleaning and cooking.

At first, I was bored and didn't like this at all. I then started developing an interest in baking. I tried my hand at making dinner for my family every Sunday. I thoroughly enjoyed it.

I have always loved baking but never found the time. Lockdown gave me a chance to bake.
At first, my cakes were a disaster. I also messed up the entire kitchen! Slowly, I became more organized. My cakes and cookies turned out to be tastier and much more edible.

Lockdown taught me quite a few things. Being independent was one. In lockdown many people lost their jobs, they lost all their income. Many of them even lost hope. That was sad. Because of COVID - 19 people are spending more time with family. They are giving time to their hobbies and much more. I have seen many people having faith and looking at the positive side of things.

I realized that no matter what life throws at you, you should be able to find a way out. Due to lockdown, most people weren't able to do their daily exercise. Now many have started with online classes. There are online tuitions, online yoga classes, virtual schooling, and whatnot. Everyone found a way out.

One good thing about all this was that I got to play a lot of video games and watch a surprising amount of television. Overall the experience wasn't bad but wasn't too good either.

SELF-DATE

Tejaswini Agrawal

"Beneath the Mongolian tree, I started making a tent. Some tough wooden sticks, ice cream, fluffy pillow and scented mattress were all I needed. Distracted by some of the chirping birds, singing in unison the sound of peace and gleam, I was self-musing in the twilight. Grabbing some of the munchies, a glass of potent wine and caramelized chocolate fudge, my first self-date made me over the moon.

Cherishing the glimpse, I painted the Canvas with strokes of Introspection. The ironical painting portrayed a tangling heart, filled with scars and bleak. Holding upon this heavy burden of disappointments, my fingers were lacking the strength. Increasingly the emptiness and despondent got thicker. But somehow, winds switched, grass seemed greener and nature looked optimistic. That was the spell white filament of desire rose from soil of agony, and I discerned.

It's just about taking an initiative, a decision or a perspective to remove the glitch and bloom flower of self-love within. And this lockdown teaches me to prioritize and love one's self first."

QUARANTINE: THE SEPARATION

Nikita Yadav

"No real college, No real friends.
Reading lots, Face time calls.
Thinking thoughts,
Being enclosed inside the walls.
Keeping a six feet distance,
Wearing masks and washing hands,
We need to show persistence,
And stay on our own lands.
Food being delivered,
Becoming lonely
No one come to our home,
And we can't go anywhere.
Money also been used after sanitizing,
And vegetables which come to our home we should wash them regularly.
We should get a lot of time,
To learn a lot and make our talent shine.
Hopefully these days will never again,
Soon we should get out of this quarantine,
To spread out wings in open sky, to fly high.
This is temporary period come to teach you the meaning of separation,
To build a healthy and beautiful relationship.

NEW NORMAL

Mugdha Daware

Hey there,
It all started from March 2020,
Unknown words came into picture which was just known
to dictionary;
Total lockdown in country, state, city,
Doors closed, and we were just with our family;
Every small thing was closed,
It was the time that we all explored;
There was a lot frustration and depression,
Everyone found a way follow your passion;
People started working for the community,
Oh wait,
We also had a beautiful glimpse of humanity;
For progress, we shifted to urban places,
But this situation made us realize,
Rural ones are the safest;
We were told to maintain distance physically,
We learned to be habitual with #new normal happily.

QUARANTINE: AN EYE OPENING EXPERIENCE

Keerthana Suriya

At first, I thought it's not easy to get
Through the quarantine alone. I hated it
But then I realized it is the best time
To pick up things I'm good at and things
Which I couldn't do in my busy schedule.
We always confuse "being alone" with "being lonely"
But there is a huge difference.
Being alone doesn't necessarily cause loneliness.
Actually being alone is sometimes important for our well-being.
I realized this during quarantine.
It helped me to explore the possibilities of life.
It gave an opportunity to learn
And realize more about myself.
It boosted my creativity and most importantly
I started to prioritize self-care and self-love
It was an eye-opening experience.

LOCKED INSIDE

Jyoti Dhima

"It's time to realize that
How important family is?
Lockdown opened the door of home
Earlier it was only rest house.
And I was the earning machine.
Running to fetch my unending well of greed neglecting
my health
And lovely moments with my family,
I was not fully alive and forget my sense of being alive.

It's time to realize
How important family is?
Now Spending Little moments
With my growing champ, Adorable daughter
And lovable old mom, sharing their dreams
Playing and allowing them to win liberally
As my little princess dances when wins
My champ tries to win by cheating,
Fighting a lot with each other
Granny teaches them that winning
is not always important.

It's time to realize

How important family is?
In these moments, financially tight
But heart is   finding it's peace and light
I found my dirt laden diary hidden
In storeroom with trash, Treasuring
These memories forever in my diary
Although Things will not remain same
Soon we will overcome this corona phase
But learnt a lesson for always...

It's time to realize
How important is family is?

QUARANTINE: A LESSON

Owais Khursid Bhat

"Quarantine a time which made me realize about how others live.
Quarantine a time which shaped my life,
Quarantine a time in which I got to know how poor people live,
Quarantine a time which showed me what real life is,
Quarantine a time that made me more health conscious,
Quarantine a time which told me why health is wealth,
Quarantine a time which made me angry as I had no contact with outside world.
Quarantine toughest time,
Quarantine taught a great lesson of how to care for others"

THE SUDDEN OUTBREAK

Teertha Unni

"It started like having a piece of cake, Became the sudden outbreak,
Some people say its fake,
Some people can't afford to make that mistake,

The virus contained all of us,
Instead of us containing the virus,
Those who aren't affected make a big fuss,
While others fall under the bus,

The quarantine made us whole,
The lockdown took a toll,
The pandemic made us take a call,
On whether or not the virus is a blessing in disguise at all,

We've learnt about how to be,
When the world is worth it to see,
How we were brought down to one knee,
Not realizing that everything that
Happened this year was our future key,

The feeling of remorse we can't shake, Lessons that are valuable to us we take,
Realizing that nothing was fake,
At the end, it was all just a piece of cake."

LOCKDOWN LESSONS

Leslin Shusma D'Souza

2020, the nightmare, is finally a thing of the past.
We're officially in a new year now,
But has the storm really passed?
Can we safely say we're out of the woods?
That we've dodged the proverbial bullet?

For me, the past year has been a learning experience.
Lessons in patience, humility, kindness,
Surrendering yourself to the higher power,
Hoping you'll see light at the end of your tunnel,
That it'll all work out in your favor,
Hope that the tears shed are not in vain

Work, career, goals, important no doubt,
But friends, family, loved ones matter so much more,
'Cos when you have no one else to turn to,
It's your loved ones who help you raise once more.

So let's welcome this New Year
With a bright smile on our face
And renewed hope in our hearts.

GRATITUDE

S Suganthi

Gratitude for this year...
For the isolation, for it has allowed me time and space
To observe within.
For the insanity via the media and news,
For it has brought me into a deeper curiosity
To ask hard questions and seek solutions.
For the perceived & persistent threat of this pandemic,
For it has brought me in closer contact with
What truly matters in life?
Despite all the challenges that these times are offering up,
My wish is for us all to find moments of stillness,
Quiet and gratitude for all of life's offerings;
The beauty, the contrast, and everything.

STAY AWAY

Santhi Anandan

Stay away to save yourself
Stay away to save your family
Stay away to save your relatives
Stay away to save your friends
Stay away to save your neighbors
Stay away to save your community
Stay away to save your country
Stay away even from touching yourself
Stay away social distancing to be alive
“STAY AWAY TO STAY SAFE”
Stays Corona virus adamantly stating
Silently threatening the whole world
Else, "I AM YOURS FOREVER".

2020: MY PRODUCTIVE YEAR

Pragya Verma

My quarantine life in 2020 was not so good and not so bad,
I was sometimes happy or sometimes sad.
Living with family still suffered from loneliness,
As my mind was surrounded by darkness,
That sucked my spark and made me blind,
But still I managed to conquer my mind.
Everyone said you are this, you are that,
In their hate, I don't know when i got trapped.
Because of their hateful vibes, I lost myself,
But now I stopped listening to them, and i don't give a damn,
Because I started loving the person i am.
Loving myself as much as I can,
As now, my life's new phase began.
I started focusing on my inner talents,
Pushed myself to face new challenges.
Earlier, 2020 was so devastating,
But, now I feel it helped us a lot to learn and grow,
And to pull ourselves out of our comfort zone.

SEALED BOXES

M Dhivya

The sight Blurred with darkness,
Scared of loneliness,
Locked inside boxes.

The shackles that bonded,
Society to our doorstep,
Is retreating somewhere,
Unknown before our eyes.

Though times are challenging
There's awaited personal space
But behind these doors
There's only frightening sorrow
This echoes for old times once again.

ONE AMONG OTHERS

Shivkumar K V

Fear gripped humane, in corpus of frustration.
Families locked self, through disgusting pandemic.
Hope is only the four walls, for the human renaissance.
For once in every century, it appeared again and again;
The bloody and fleshy diseases,
Cholera or Corona; Black Death or Spanish flu;
Made many breathless and vanish.
There, men alerted inner engineering;
Pushed out the trauma within.
Hope may not be of sins; Hope may not be a curse.
Cheered the Medics; hugged the Scavengers;
Felicitated the Doctors; Saluted the Cop.
Wished by sounds and tinkling;
For the bravery and being Gods of the Age.
Stayed at home; as one among others;
And others for everyone.
May be, a day comes, of not being human centric;
But part of the Nature's citadel.

THE BATTLE OF COVID-19

Sakshi Somani

"Once in a century, comes a global pandemic,
Tougher the times, greater the learning's,
Finding that little ray of positives,
In a cloud of negatives,
Will be your rescue mentally and emotionally,
Life will keep throwing lemons at us; one after the other, problems will keep coming,
But it is up to us about how we opened the door of creative solution,
Situation turned from rainbow and colours to thunder and lightning,
History is being written, and we are going to be the characters of the textbook,
No trace of life on the empty streets, everyone is on house arrest,
Health care workers fighting against the unwelcomed monster,
The war is still rolling, our warriors are still on the battlefield,
The villain of our story will not triumph, as our heroes are still fighting with their superpowers,
The least we can do as loafers to the tussle, is wear a mask and take precautions,
Because the fight isn't over yet,
And we will not give up until the death of the monster.

LUMBERING DAYLIGHTS

Dinesh S R

Laziness call my sun to turn as the moon of dawn -
Oscillating tone from days and breaks with a yawn.
Cajoling my mind to push myself towards a cot,
Killing my thumbs whilst the mobile turns hot.
Deferring my limbs as to step out of the walls,
Obsessed with my friends when they make calls.
Wrestling with my mom for foods and stuffs, and
Nagging cuffs which ruins my days with toughs.

Through gallons of stress one's temper might lose
Owed by anxiety, I turned on my skills to ooze.
Hectic days that put off my respites are now gone,
Enticing myself to un-hide my talents and put on -
Admired to paint, trials on food, drawn to movies,
Valuing folks whilst my inert writer gains to unleash.
Ever not tried of such ecstasy to fancy those days
Neither to dwell with, nor to resume olds just in case.

THE COVID-19 LOCKDOWN

Radneswary Sooriyakumar

"It was a sudden stop
The whole world was paused
Not for a minute or two
But for months.

Behind the doors
Started a new journey
Where everyone
Started to discover them.

Initially everyone complained
And was worried
Calling it a curse
Though their heart enjoyed it.

It was the break
Which everyone were longing for
From a very long time.
And they loved this boon.

A break from the fast moving world
To spend some time with their
Loved ones - All thanks
To COVID.

THE CAGED STUDENTS

Zainab Abid

"I remember the beginning how we all thought this was gonna last just a few weeks, just like that those few weeks turned to months and from that it's been over a year but the situation remains the same. This quarantine has affected each and every person either physically or mentally and maybe even both.

The online classes or the work from home has destroyed us mentally and let's not get into how this quarantine has affected us physically.

People doing work from home or online classes I believe each one of us has heard this "" you're at home only. Why are you tired?""

Working people have increased work load, each and every student is stressed. Two batches of 10th were passed without boards, they are being labeled as lucky. Why? Because they don't have to write exams but you know what those same students did not get a farewell, they had to spent what was supposed to be their last school year at home but every person has the audacity to say how lucky those students are in my opinion they are very unfortunate and they are not at fault it is this pandemic that has moved the world.

I believe every student who reads this will agree how hard online studies have been, it has been the same for those students whose exams were just cancelled. People have lost their jobs, families were separated, the economy has taken a hit and most importantly Millions of people have lost their lives and yet we are still joking around.

This pandemic has been hard on everyone so let's not be too quick to judge and acknowledge our problems and find a solution and the solution is not jokes, unwanted comments or questions in fact it is acknowledgement and understanding.

JAUNT OF PIVOTAL PROMPTS

Musaib Bashir

Through the Mirror I stare consistently at surrounding
with Corpse hope of getting into it,
The way everything is staggeringly delightful, crunches
me to snap Aid out of it.
Being isolated from my own fellows is the first wretched
experience me going with,
Teaches me the eminence of family in every moment I am
scrolling with.
Though the pain of 100k people suffering from same draw
a blank to me from my Misery,
Realizes me the Sensitive nature arising all over in the
society.
It's the only Moment I get ample of time to get in touch
with exploring knowledge of books so far,
Nothing less nothing more I go through series of write-
ups, pump lets in this out breaking bar.
Taking all the precautions, preventions I'm thriving
towards satisfactory health,
I want to urge my people sanitize well, stay in home at
maximum, step out with mask, and take very possible
care of your health.

ENDOWMENTS OF LOCKDOWN

Jyoti Gogia

In the sequester of my study, I found
My solivagant soul that was lost in me
Like phosphine emerges in murky dungeon
I broke the shackles of limited vision.

Ebbing away from the disdain world
Lockdown brought an aurora seraphic
Glare that pushed under layers of time
Solemnly metamorphosed in lockdown.

While masses were exigent of escaping out
Irate they were, felt sick and stressed
My insanity for scribbling pen to write
The poetess invaded again in tranquility.

Long days that I had spent in nothingness
Scribe was concealed under foggy mist
Candid words are strung as tassel
Festoon lines soak up all the worries.

Rudiment of a new version of mine
Fills up the precipice of monotony
Obnoxious thoughts of self-abhor quit
Lockdown endowed me trinket of poetry.

HEY CORONA

Saumili Dutta

It's 2021 and I spent these 16 months staying at home. Last year when exams were cancelled we felt grateful but we never realized that how difficult it'll be getting admission in colleges.

When you brought the families together, we thanked you but we never thought how we will spend the following days then. Financial conditions were tight.

It was because of you that India made new record. Remember last year second last week of March and April? Pollution level was decreasing, ozone layer was healing, lazy peeps were becoming lazier, some started writing, and some took this time for self-improvement. Cases decreased. I went out with my friends during Durga Puja. Crowds were less dense.

I started feeling that everything is going to be alright, when scientists discovered your relatives in different countries and my test report was positive.

The first week was the laziest week of my life, I was weak. The only thing I did was lie on my bed and stare. Stare at the ceiling, stare at stars and moon. I couldn't sleep much. Second week I started reading. Reading stories online.

Once my results were negative I continued writing and blogging, I learnt how to cook and made my own secret recipes. My write-ups got published in anthologies. I learnt guitar and took classes in different courses.

Since last week of March, Gosh! Cases were raising so much. Even people who thought that this virus was just a political propaganda were having panic attacks. We, the teenagers, we feel like our life is destroyed, we are so depressed about future. Employees of private organizations are also worried about their family.

ISOLATED MEMORIES

Jasmine Parveen

"These days, coronavirus locked people,
That feels like we are locked in a cage,
A home like a cage,
Roads are scary,
Faces are scared.
Can't say when it's gonna end,
But all I want is to flap my wings back to school again,
I want to touch the books in the library again,
I want to dust off the dirt from my bench again
I want to share my tiffin box again.
I want to go mountains and all my favorite places
I'm done with the responsibilities of being careless,
Why have we gone off the mask shamelessly?
Was it hard for us to control?
I guess life deserved to be treated as a gift,
Humans should understand that God won't come again and again to lift us.
Don't you want to run on the grassy ground again?
Let's hope for better days,
Let's come together to help people who are searching for their heroes,
Quarantine would be the best help,
Treat yourself as it's the last day you have.
Follow the rules and make sure you are breathing to dream again.

FOREVER IN OUR HEART

Nirali U Potdar

The day that was not less than occasion for her,
She was going to be the mother.
Message that she sent to everyone,
Two little steps after some months will make her home
beautiful.
Excitement of the baby shower function had she,
But the disease "Corona" stole her happiness.
Never had she thought of being hospitalized for it,
But fought bravely with it till her last breath.
Sadly, my dear sister left all of us from this world,
But forever you will be alive in our heart.
Miss you.

LOCKDOWN AND ONLINE LIFE

Akshat Goyal

As the lockdown begin in the
23 March's morning shine
We can see
The life become online
Few become lazy
And few at home had gone crazy

The aim just lead
To none other than
Stop this Poisonous Covid 19 weed
This has grown worst for man
As asked Lockdown by WHO of UN
To safeguard the life of every men.

Addicted to Phone and being online
That some has made its use
Even it at the time of dine
This is truth, you can't refuse.
If the non-working of internet goes
Then the mind of few off blows

Few uses for good deed
This is productive
Few as bad lead
Depicting it constructive
It all depends on you
Which type of use you chew?

THE BLINK OF BLUE

Tanupreet Kaur

Everything was just normal, ever since we born,
Without a clue, for years we are going to mourn.
We did not know, such flourished population,
Would run for survival of the fittest competition.

Happy faces, joyful rides and lovely moments,
Just in the blink of eye turned into no amusement.
All plans we had for the bright future,
Now started seeming difficult to nurture.

We were living for the utmost luxury,
Till the time we realized, forgot ample of necessary.
The gap of rich and poor not only existed,
Even widened during the time of quarantined.

We took all the essentials for granted,
For which we are now continuously ranted.
We realized the worth of being alive,
When day by day it is becoming tough to save a life.

REFLECTION OF DARKNESS

Priyanka Parsia Sur

I run the mad rat race,
Keeping pace ahead of time
People buzzing around me everywhere
Scramble; awkwardly fill gaps within their lives.
Success, fortune and fame,
We choose over family, love, comrade,
When suddenly the chaotic world halts still,
As Terror - the fatal fear masked Pandemic outbreaks.
Breathlessness, headaches, Sleepless nights
Body aches, Pneumonia, Anxiety - Will I survive?
So naive was I to miss out on precious moments of my life,
Quarantined indoors, lockdown outside – Tumble upon a new insight.

Embrace your today, for bygones are gone
Celebrate relationships, knitting miracles anew,
Slow down, be grounded, Live mindfully without regrets
Recall thy blessings; Make space for your passion, your dreams.

Lessons to remember, did I learn in my darkest hours,
Live life to the fullest, for everyone comes with a shelf-life.